Content

The follow lessons in this booklet are part of MARS 13 subject mental and economic development workshop to help develop individual self improvement.

Introduction

I'm a born hustler and proud of it! People seem to think being a hustler is about manipulating people and in some cases, this is true. Earlier in life I felt the same way, until I acquired different perceptions about acceptable, expectable and respectable hustle.

A hustler is a state of mine, it is just another way to describe an ambitious entrepreneur. In my 15 years of experience in entrepreneurship and hustling, I've learned that there is no difference between a hustler and an ambitious businessperson. The goal of both is to acquire products or services at the lowest price and sell them at a higher price. The goal in business is to hustle, or in other words, to sell products or services. This is what's accepted, expected and respected

Most businesses have what is called "SALES Tactics." A sales tactic is when products and service prices are reduced to sell, promote, or to closely break even on cost. In most cases, the price was raised months or weeks before the sale and then reduced to the original cost. This is done to manipulate the consumer into thinking they are saving money. The product was put on sale because sales ratios were down. Truth is the company could have sold it at the sale price from the beginning. The word "sale" is about the hustle in order to make as must profit as possible. This is accepted, expected and respected manipulation called good business practice.

Every business has to have someone to sell its product or service. The sales people are the backbone of the operation. The true salesman is a hustler. When I think of a salesman, I reflect back to when I first got in the car business in 1996. The sales manager was named Terrence Harris, BKA "T". I didn't fully recognize it then, but T was one of the best salesmen I've ever had the privilege of working with. I would away tell him I wanted to be as good as he was. One day T Harris was consulting me about a sale that I was having difficulty with. In the middle of the conversation he asked me, "what do you want to do with your life and

50 Things to Know

We'd love to hear what you think about our content! Please leave your honest review of this book on Amazon and Goodreads. We appreciate your positive and constructive feedback. Thank you.

Knowledge I Belief I Ambition I Motivation I Persistence

NATURAL
BORN

HUSTLE

"Learn To Sell Your Natural Abilities"
A Young Entrepreneur Need To Read Booklet

Written By

Hillery Marcellus Scott

Illustrations By Ernie Augurson

For More On Info. www. marcellusscott.com

Disclaimer

The information in this booklet is basic knowledge and is not to be used as an absolute but an intermediate and unconventional learning tool. It is displayed to inspire an individual's will to research and seek higher levels of advancement in order to achieve goals. I'm not an accredited professional or an authorized authority on these following subjects. My credibility comes from real life experience, science and research. I recommend additional research on any basic subject matter.

Hillery Marcellus Scott
Writer & Publisher
Marcellusscott.com

A **MARS** Project

Editorial Support

Ms.Gloria Dean Elzy
Demeshia Williams
John Lacarbiere III
Aja Anderson
Michelle Brown

For information and online article visit
marcellusscott.com

If you're just starting a small business, more than likely, you're working more hours for yourself than you would work for an employer; due to a lack of affordable help. To keep up with your business production and make more profit, you work longer hours for yourself. This is somewhat the same when working for an employer. You work over time for the demand of your employer's company, which increases company production and makes more profit. This makes you more money, because of bonuses and incentives as an employee. Whether you're an employer or employee, "It's all about ambition and hustle"

Ambitious Cycle

I've noticed that sometimes in life it seems that no matter what you do you seem to fail. We keep making the same mistakes over and over. We repeat the same type of relationships, jobs, people, friends, and stress. This creates the question; "Why is this happening?" This type of behavior haunted me for years. I felt I always had the knowledge of what to do. I would ask, "GOD why is this happening to me?" "Why can't make life work for me?" I prepare, start, and end with the same results, all the while looking for a magic solution from GOD, or from anywhere it could come from. I was not getting an answer, or at least that's what I thought. Little did I know that I was given the answer how to be successful through the gift of my talents, but I did just like a lot of others do; I listened but didn't obey. I listened more to my doubts and fears which led to a lot of other unproductive thoughts that created a feeling of failure.

When things don't go as planned, most people start thinking, "everything happens for a reason" or "it was meant to be". After every perception of failure, our minds continue to remember what we were first told to do but didn't do. In the end we say, "I should have followed my first mind." Our beginning thoughts are our seed thoughts or success path, which require focus and action.

21 Ambitious Lessons

I have put together 21 very simple lesson that I've learned from my past experiences to help inspire the ambition within yourself and build motivation while on your path to self-improvement

Lesson 1
Stop Procrastinating
Get Started

Avoid procrastination at all costs; it is one of the main causes of failure. Start doing what you want to do. It doesn't matter what you decide to do, just get started. Stop putting off today for tomorrow and always take the opportunity in the present. Also, remember that nothing is certain in a future unseen.

Lesson 2
Don't Let A lack Of Money Stop You

We need money to do just about everything in this life, but in no way should it stop you from getting started. The fact is, money starts and ends with your actions. It's important to understand that most success starts from the bottom and works its way to the top. When you have a lack of money, it's the best time to take action because there is more inspiration in your work. When you are at your lowest, you really need to succeed the most. That fact alone should push you to work harder for success. In other words, "you're hungry for it," so you focus more on trying to be successful and you are less inclined to waste time. It's all about the effort.

Lesson 3
Don't Let A lack Of Knowledge Stop You

Research and Learn Enough to
"GET STARTED"
"Life Will Work Out The Detail."

It's a fact that it's not necessary to totally understand something to be able to use it. I don't believe that I have to get bogged down in every detail. I have studied leaders in my community and found that they have working knowledge on numerous subjects; however, they do not know every detail of the inner workings of those subjects.

Lesson 4
Don't Fear Rejection

One of the most powerful words in the human language is two letters, "NO." To keep moving and to be successful at taking actions, you must learn how to handle rejection so that the fear of the word "NO" no longer lowers your energy and stops you from taking actions. Most successful people are those who have been rejected the most. They are the ones who can take the word "NO" and use it as a symbol to continue. "No is just an answer, it's not the end."

For More On Info. www. marcellusscott.com

Lesson 5
Do What You Love
The True Meaning of Successful

'The secret of success is making your vocation your vacation.'
-Mark Twain-

The smartest way you can ever work is doing what you love. Successful and ambitious people are ones that are doing what they love doing, and getting paid for it. It's about linking what you're paid to do and what you love to do freely. Making your vocation your vacation, that's what successful people seem to do. What most people love doing is called their hobby and while hobbies don't normally involve making money or unwanted work tasks, it does involve passion and true skill that leads to success..

Lesson 6
Create A Brand
"Name, term, design, symbol, or feature that identifies one product distinction from others."
It's What Most Successful Ambitious People Have?

How To Brand Yourself?
Everybody wants to be with winners, so always show it in your attitude or presence. By showing a winning attitude, you will brand yourself in the mind of people as a winner. Unfortunately, if you feel like a loser, that will brand also.

For More On Info. www. marcellusscott.com

Most people and parents have a lot of respect for kids who are trying to better themselves. They understand that there's no long-lasting success without work. The way to succeed is to be confident with work and attitude.

We've all noticed when celebrities come around they get most things free, even if they have the money to pay. They get what they want because they represent success. The same can work for you as well, by just showing your hustle and people will treat you with respect, and that is your brand. All of the following lessons are forms of branding as well.

Lesson 7
Create A Plan
Put your goals on paper

To get where you want to be, it is effective to have a map to guide yourself. Take a little time to make a map of your trip to success.

Plans are projections, not the outcome. All outcomes don't reveal positive results; but that doesn't give you a reason not to plan. . We all have heard the statement "if you don't plan, you plan to fail." Plans are the belief systems of your journey that will create commitments to your goals.

Lesson 8
Hustle Legally
Don't try To Ice Skate Up Hill

Don't seek success illegally, the odds are against you. There are thousands of ways to hustle legally by using your talents and skills with today's technologies. If you're currently hustling illegally, then improve your conditions and discontinue the illegal activity. Take from your benefits and give to others to help improve their conditions and for all the crime you have committed, give twice as much to others. To commit a crime, it takes ambition and effort, so why not be just as ambitious legally as you would illegally. Doing crime for money is an illegal business and in the business criminal world you have to buy and sell illegal products or services at the risk of your freedom. People in a legal business have to buy, sell, and distribute legal products or services at the risk of their money, time, energy and efforts. The biggest difference between being legal and illegal is, when you legally hustle; there's only chance of losing your money and lifestyle. With illegal hustle, you have a chance of losing not only your money and lifestyle, but your freedom as well. Why take a chance of losing your freedom or life when it isn't necessary?

With True Hustle, Crime Is Unnecessary

What I'm about to reveal I don't recommend to anyone, but it's my history and I hope by writing this it will give you inspiration to be motivated to hustle legally if you're into illegal hustling. I've always been a hard worker, not because I like to work but because of the need for money.

In the 90's if you weren't working fast food the only hustle for young black individuals with a lack of economic knowledge was crime. I wasn't an exception to that. I went from job to job trying to make as much money as I could. I ran into an old friend from high school named Greg White. He was a good friend and a born hustler. He introduced to me what's known on the street as "Torking." Torking is professionally known as white-collar crime. He taught me things I will not mention, out of respect for him. I will say that it gave me the attitude and belief that jobs were for suckers. People that have experienced fast money usually feel this way until they realize that crime pays, but at the cost of freedom. I committed white-collar crime for over 10 years with nothing to show for it but knowledge, memories, and no stability. With respect of the truth, I'm not saying that all illegal hustling doesn't end with stability or a happy ending, but I don't know any that have. Just as some legal hustlers end with no stability as well. They are no guarantees legally or illegally, but I recommend all things legal because guaranteed freedom is better than possible jail.

Lesson 9
Promote Yourself Daily

Everyone has a skill to sale such as singing, dancing, drawing, cooking, etc. It doesn't matter what talent you have, it can be sold for profit. The main objective is focus, dedication, and commitment to your natural abilities. True hustle, is to sale your natural legal abilities. .

Lesson 10
Learn What Is Needed

The best way to gain power is to get the knowledge you need to be more effective. There are many ways to get knowledge, and the most common way is to go to school by way of grants and loans. I believe the easiest way to gain knowledge is by researching information over the internet or at the library. There is no excuse not to have knowledge in this new information age. You can search the internet on virtually any subject, and within seconds there are thousands of sources on anything you want to know. If you don't have a computer, there is local Internet access available at libraries, restaurants, and community centers in your area. Being that there is an endless source of knowledge available, "There Is No Excuse!"

For More On Info. www. marcellusscott.com

The Job Race

It is a fact, when someone finishes high school; it is not enough jobs to employ every young person that is available for work. The ratio of available jobs compared to youth available for employment, averages 5 jobs to every 50 employable grad from high school or college. When it comes to high wage jobs, the average is 60% lower in lower income areas. Looking at the average working adult citizen, there are hardly enough jobs that allow for a decent living that supports the world's changing economy.

There is also a lack of graduate economic employment programs that would create job opportunities for the unemployed graduate. It is very important to sell yourself as much as possible to win in the race for employment.

Lesson 11
Learn To Create A Job

How many times have you said to yourself, "I need to go look for a job"? Most of the time, that's what you ended up doing; looking and not finding. It would be best to create a plan for 'job negotiation.' It's important to remember to think of the word "No" as negotiation. You need to find out where you want to work and create a plan to negotiate for it. You can get knowledge and get paid at the same time by doing a work internship with a local business in your area. There are a lot of businesses in your area that need volunteers. This will give you a chance to start on-the-job training and gain education at the same time. This also gives you a chance for future employment with that company or you can at the very least, use it as a job reference. An added benefit of being a volunteer is that it exposes you to different people and experiences, which equips you with a better insight of what your interests are.

When I moved to a city from a rural area I didn't know much, but I had one important factor: I have always had strong ambition. Even though my current financial situation didn't show much promise, I had the drive and determination to be successful. My motivation and persistence gave me the ability to get a lot of different jobs that I actually wanted. My sister would ask, "How are you getting all the good jobs". My only reply was, "Hustle." I was always searching for different opportunities. While my parents felt that I was being irresponsible, I felt it was just another way of getting my hustle on. Throughout my entire job hopping process, there is this one job that I remember well. It changed the way I looked at job hunting. I will share this experience with you.

When I moved to Dallas in 1995, I had a job cleaning office buildings at night. Roosevelt Owens, my brother-in-law gave me this opportunity to assist me in establishing myself. At that point in my life, I would have worked any job that paid me.

I then got a second job cleaning office buildings during the day. I was focused on working hard, and I was convinced that I was going to be successful. The night job provided security income to pay bills and to help in getting my own apartment. Income from my day job was for career savings and advancement. The problem I faced was that I had no time to go and search for new opportunities because all of my time was filled with working. It became clear to me I had to make some sacrifices. I decided to quit my day job cleaning office buildings and replace it with a job toward my future career.

I had a passion for graphic designs, plus I had some intermediate personal work experience in that field. I was limited in job experience so it was difficult to get hired. I knew that if I could just start doing graphics for a company, it would be the key to getting started in professional graphics. Eventually, I came up with a plan to get a job in computer graphics. I located a very credible advertising agency and offered my services to the company for free part-time, in order to learn additional graphic design skills. This was a sacrifice I made for my future career. It was also my way of self-education to achieve my goals.

I have witnessed other people, as well as myself, that have gone to college to get a job in certain career fields. They too had to intern for free to learn and gain work creditability. I decided I would do the same, but the only difference was, I wasn't in school. I understood that a college degree is mainly about educational creditability, so I decided to create my own credibility. I knew that building creditability meant getting noticed for your education and work. I worked free with dedication as a volunteer for about six months and I did the best job I could. I worked harder than anyone else in the company. I came to work on time, did as I was told and showed dedication on all tasks. I monitored all company needs and wants and offered my assistance. By working hard and showing dedication, I learned all the advantages and disadvantages in the company's workflow and I became proficient with company management. I was so good at what I did there, eventually, I realized how I was the only one who could trouble shoot the company's workflow issues.

I helped improved company productivity for six months. At the end of six months, I gave my 30-day notice to end my volunteer work. I left that advertising agency with the knowledge to go work for other advertising agencies. I was able to get new jobs with other advertising agencies, because I used the previous volunteer job as a reference. The big difference was I was able to get paid because of my previous on- the- job experience. I was paid well enough that I didn't have to work two jobs anymore and was able to leave my night job. Surprising, the previous advertising agency that I volunteered with wanted me to come back and work for them full-time with full salary and benefits. The supervisor stated the reason he offered me a job with such a high salary, was because my work performance was noticed and appreciated. He also stated that in my absence, the company's workflow decreased. They looked at me as an important asset to the company. They offered to pay me more money than the people working there with college degrees. The point of this story is, "You can do what you want or don't want; the choice is yours, but you have got to make sacrifices for what you want."

Lesson 12

Use and Sell Your Resources

Resources are all around us in the form of knowledge, money, people and opportunities to name a few. We must take advantage of them to get ahead in life. These resources can be useful in any environment filled with people that possess below average education or people with money. Everyone has resources; the key is to notice them and apply them effectively.

You're An Affective & Effective Resource

Be a productive tool that can be a resource to others. Everyone has skills and can be creative with them. Most people don't use their skills effectively in order to meet their needs or the needs of others. As I stated earlier, people are your greatest resource and also the key to your success. There is someone who has what you need or the ability to help you get what you want. I know you've heard the statement "Give the People What They Want". It's all about finding out the needs of people and supplying them with it.

Everything you want in life is owned and spread out among people. To receive, you have to give of yourself. Most people can't function properly

and is made of magnets also. When two magnets get close to each other mentally or physically they attract. If you get close to what you want and it will attract to you. You can attract your dreams by following all previous lessons.

Lesson 18
Become An Entrepreneur

When I first heard the word entrepreneur I had no idea what it meant. Like a lot of young people in small rural areas, I was clueless of the things that apply to business. The only word that made sense to me was 'money.' Man, was I wrong!

As I stated in my opening introduction, an entrepreneur is someone who exercises personal initiative. In other words, entrepreneur is another word for ambition. They're people who organize a venture and take advantage of opportunities. They are also the decision makers that decide who, what, when, where and how much in situations.

Most people feel that being an entrepreneur is all about having a business of selling products and services. It's really about handling your business at home, work, and in business. You basically have to be a productive ambitious person in your everyday life. Entrepreneurs seek opportunities like employees seek jobs, and employers seek workers.

Lesson 19
Learn Basic Money Management

Money management starts by understanding what money is. Money is an object or record used as payment for goods, services and repayment of debts. The main functions of money are distinguished as: The level of exchange, a unit of account, and occasionally the standard of deferred payment.

Money has changed numerous times in the past. Money was first introduced as a trading tool for metal, gold, silver, and copper. Later coins were substituted with paper money, which is what we have today. As gold and silver were collected, safe keeping became difficult. There was a need for locations to reserve money and handle transactions better. These areas became known as money reserves (banks.) Just as now, banks would store the citizen's money and give them legal paper exchanges called notes. Notes were given for the amount that was kept in a bank account. These notes were known as "owe you notes."

The easiest way to understand this is by looking at the way we use our current checking accounts. Most citizens deposit paper money into the banks and are given checks to do financial transactions. The use of money has transformed to using credit cards, debit cards, and computerized mobile transactions. The exchange of money has changed according to the needs and availability of society.

For More On Info. www. marcellusscott.com

Types of Money

Commodity Money: Gold, silver, copper and other precious metals

Fiat Money: Represents value. A standard of money that is used for what something considered valuable; otherwise known as "a legal tender".

Fiduciary Money: Known as a grantee, trust or "middle man" for a business or person. Money of two or more parties placed in the bank for safe keeping

Commercial Money: Line of Credit: Commercial Bank money or people deposits that can be used for the purchase of goods and services

Money Supply

Money supply is usually measured as four escalating categories M0, M1, M2 and M3.

M1 is (coins and bills) and checking account deposits.

M2 is currency, checking account deposits plus savings account deposits.

M3 is **M2** plus the time of deposits (the flow of money)

M0 is base money or the actual amount of money in the centralized bank of a country. It is measured as currency plus deposits
One fact about money is that it was made to circulate, and its principle

value remains the same. Money is just a piece of paper that's exchanged for things we feel are valuable. Money is only valuable if we have something of value to link it with, such as convenience and necessities.

Almost everyone I've ever come in contact with is trying to get, manage, and keep money in all different forms for fear of loss. Remember, money is made to circulate with risk factors impacted by earnings and management.

Money Is Always At Risk! You Are Trying To Earn, Manage, Or Save It!

Money Is Earned By:

WORKING FOR IT - Mental and physical labor risks

ASKING FOR IT - Ask for donations, charity, sponsors, or loans at risk

TAKING IT - Taking advantage of opportunity that's available to you at risk.

Money Is Managed By:

SPENDING 70% - To consume life to manage time and effort and responsibilities

SAVE 20% - To accumulate growth. You can't grow unless you add to what you have

GIVE AWAY 10% - To replenish to process by sacrifice what's important to get more.

SECURITY – Hire a lawyer and accountant to keep safe from mischief.

INVESTMENT – Funds, Business, Real estate, Commodity, Stocks, and Bonds.

INSURANCE - Precautions for unpredictable situations

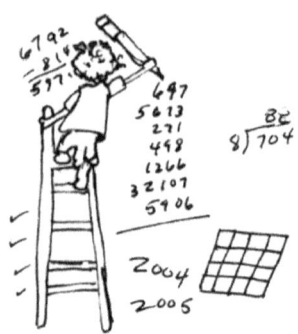

Lesson 20
Learn To Invest Spending

70% Spending

It's smart to live on 70 percent of what you have. We live in a capitalistic society surrounded by opportunity to invest. Most people are not taking advantage of those available opportunities.

Learn to spend and use your money as leverage to get more. It's called "investment spending" The purchases such as machinery, land, production devices, or infrastructure. Think investment when you buy.

For example, when you purchase, think of all products as true value. Ask yourself, if I had to sell this product later, how much would it be worth? If you buy a pair of shoes or clothing, you need to invest in the amount of time they will last. If you buy a car, you need to invest in resale value. If you buy a home, you need to invest in equity. When you buy food, you need to invest in health. You get the point. This can be applied to all purchases. If you are spending all of your earnings, with no investment, you'll never build up any value to have leverage get what you need. The bottom line is that money is like everything else; you can make it work for you or you can let it work against you. You should be able to deal with money as with anything else in your mind, with purpose and responsibility.

Your money is going to be spent no matter what, so spend it with room to save and invest. This process leaves more opportunity for future money. It reduces you from being in stressful situations that cause you to be unhappy.

For More On Info. www. marcellusscott.com

20% Saving

I know you have heard people say, "You need to save your money." To save money, you must budget and be disciplined. When you get your allowance or pay check, save some of it on a schedule; and stick with it. It doesn't matter the amount or the schedule you choose. Whatever you decide, stick with it and over time your money will add up.

10% Giving

Remember that all of our actions in life are guided by our actions. Though trial and effort, I have learned a very important key to dealing with money. Take 10 percent of all you earn up front and give it away. By doing this, you give yourself stronger reason to put back what you have taken out, which causes you to gain more. It also creates value for you and others. Most importantly it helps control your mind of greed. That's a very powerful lesson.

What you give away becomes like your starting seed when you invest. The best way to invest is to give up some of the things you acquire so that it can help others. There are people in need all around us. One of the most valuable things about giving is how it makes you feel about yourself. When you're the kind of person who inspires to fulfill the needs of others, it makes you feel differently about who you are.

I believe that people should give back a portion of what has been given to them, not because they have good character; but because it's owed. No matter how successful in life is, there's someone that helped them get there. One mistake that a lot of people make is that they feel like the things they have achieved were achieved solely by themselves. They forget about the small things that helped them along the way. Everybody owes someone or something. It's very proud feeling to know that your debts have been paid. One of the best reasons to have is to be able to help other people and pay back obligations.

For More On Info. www. marcellusscott.com

Lesson 21
"Give More Than You Expect To Receive."

I believe if you want to achieve more you have to start with giving more. Most people only want to receive first. Many times I have heard individuals say "I give and I don't get the same or anything in return." In turn I would ask, "Have you ever received anything from anyone before?" They would answer, "Well yes I have." We all have received something from someone. Maybe it was a classmate or family member, or someone you don't know. People love to measure what's given by personal survey. They expect the same or more in return, saying to themselves, "I gave so now it's your turn". It is wise not to expect the same in return because your return might not be meant to come from whom you gave to. Maybe it will return by way of someone else. Moreover, it might be returned back to you by way of your children or close family within your genetic seed.

I used to think the best way to help my family and friends was to give by doing things for them. Now I know the best way to help people is to let them know that there are other sets of choices available. My job is to help them in developing the resources to become self-sufficient. In other words, I help people by giving them information to do things for themselves.

Subject 2

Business

Self Employment & Entrepreneurship

Majority of people feel that business is all about the commercial selling of products and services. Business can be personal or business related. It's important to understand what business is really about. First it is important to mind your own personal business at home. Commercial business is about selling products and services. To start a business, you basically have to be productive and ambitious on a personal and commercial level in your everyday life.

Handle Your Business

All people have business, but some are not in control of it.

I come across many people who say they want to start a business, but they are not handling their personal business in life. They are trying to handle some ones else's. I totally understand this, because everyone including myself has been a victim of this. We try to help irresponsible adults, children, and friends

Most people are involved in other people situation 50 to 60% of their life.

People are so involved with other people issues that they feel a sense of responsibility. While they are usually handling everyone's problems and issues, they cannot recognize their own.

When you start a business, it's based on something personal that you feel is important to you. It really comes down to controlling your own personal behavior. Personal behavior includes the following: nobility, responsibility, dedication, determination, and stability. These personal subjects can make or break most personal and business endeavors

Important Note:

Business Comes From Being Busy

When you're in commercial business, you are usually busy doing business; it's all about taking responsibility. To start a commercial business, you need to understand what your business is really about. Commercial business is no different than handling personal business, such as tasks that's given around your house. We do tasks to get some value out of it that can benefit you, your family, and friends. The same applies to commercial business.

People think of how to start a business, but it's more important to understand why you want to start. You should ask yourself, "What would happen if you didn't start the business or what could happen if you did?" You could also ask, "what are the pros and cons of starting a business".

Running A Business Can Seem Complex
But Having The Right Knowledge Makes It Simple.

In order to do business, it takes time to gain the knowledge to do so. Not everyone has knowledge of the proper steps it takes. People can find many reasons why they want to start one. Those reasons whether large or small will give you the motivation to figure out how to start.

Money Is Not Always
The Answer

You may have the money to start a business, but will you take action?

"Year after year people in my community get an income tax refund but never start a business."

For More On Info. www. marcellusscott.com

I've learned that it all comes down to how you think. I've demonstrated to people how to start a small business, and some will say I'm going to get started. They later come back with a lot of excuses on why they can't. These excuses include, "I don't know how," or "no one will teach me." The excuse I hear the most often is, "no one really wants to help me." I don't mean to sound rude, but "There Are No Excuses Anymore." There is one very important tool that was invented that has made all information available right at your fingertips; the internet. This is the "World Wide Web." Information is always available.

There Are More Reasons
To Start a Business Than Not

Remember You Have One Thing
That Other Businesses
Don't And That Is,

YOU

The 10 Key Business Ethics

1. Always Pay Yourself - Pay yourself at least 20% of the profit

2. Always Advertise, Market, & Promote - It's a 70% factor in business growth, so budget 20-30% of earnings to be spent on advertising such as: Internet, TV, Newspaper, Radio Magazine, or word of mouth

3. Keep Low Overhead - Price products or services with a 100 to 300% profit mark up.

4. Always Get It In Writing - Get a signed agreement with all major jobs. "It's business not personal." Remember your business and you are separate entities. It's your baby, so protect its interest.

5. Always Cover Your Expenses Up Front
Follow the 60-40 Rule. Get 60 to 40% of the cost of doing the job up front. "No credit without credibility." Don't give credit to customers without previous experience with them.

For More On Info. www. marcellusscott.com

6. Avoid Working With Family Members - It can be a personal business liability. Your business could be taken advantage of by family members because of family obligations. Also they are also not easy to fire. This type of working relationship is a huge liability.

7. Avoid Business Complacency - "Keep Up With Technology." Invest in the things your business needs in order to cater to new customers and respect old ones. Remodel your business every 1 to 3 years.

8. Be Fast and Resourceful - It keeps you ahead in business production, and it makes your customer respect you. It shows respect toward your customers

9. Keep Your Word - If you tell your customers you're going to do something, do it. It shows reliability, truthfulness and dependability. If your customers feel you're reliable, it will give them the belief that they can count on you personally to get the job done. It also creates repeat customers.

10. Business First, Play Later

• If There Is Work To Be Done, Start On It Right Away
• If There Are Goals To Meet, Then Meet Them First
• If there's a meeting always attend. If you can't attend a meeting, call and reschedule.

There are more ethics that you can apply from many other sources that is not mentioned. These are some that I have learned from my failures, which are very essential to business stress and harmony. Use them wisely.

Making Business Work

Problems with most small businesses are that the businesses work less, but the owners work more. If you want to succeed with a small business, you must get the return you deserve by getting other people to earn it for you. As I explained earlier, nearly every failing business has the following common themes:

- The owner becomes indispensable.
- The business cannot do without them
- They are irreplaceable
- Nothing can happen without them and everything happens because of them.

What alternatively happens is the owner becomes convinced that they are not getting the returns they deserve; so they give up. It's important not to quit but reevaluate. Create your business in a way where it will not be able to do without you, but at the same time can work without you.

Every penny that your business earns that you were not involved in is "FREE MONEY."

The only way to get the return you deserve is to make sure your business and your employees are earning money for you. The difference between working for your business and your business working for you is your personal finances, and business planning. This makes a difference that is shown in your business.

Be Consistent In Business

To be consistent in your business truly relies on what your business does. If you research any great business, you will find that they all have consistent beliefs and confidence in what their business does. Look at businesses such as McDonalds, Wal-Mart and Sears. The customers know what to expect, the products are consistent, the business area is the same, the parking lot looks the same, and the stores look the same. This is all due to consistency.

Time Is Money

It's important to understand that time is a tool for your business as well as your money. They are both used to do things in business. Money is spent, invested, and contributed. Time is contributed within products through labor. The time it takes to produce, manage, and sale a product or service is time and resources that can't be replaced. Time is a very valuable asset, and should be respected and sold.

Ask yourself, how much is your time worth?

If you really got paid for your time, what are you truly worth? How much more money would you have? Truthfully, one's self-worth is without measure, so it's very difficult to truly get the amount of money that you deserve. You only get the return you deserve by getting other people to earn it for you. Hiring people to work for you is how you create free time.

Free Time

There are people in this world made to be followers, workers, and to be controlled. These are your laborers. They will work for less pay or free with the promise of reward. It is a concept of "selling the dream" As I stated earlier, everyone has a dream. They are either living it by being in control or being controlled.

Selling a dream it about what you say and show, which can be an effective way to build an illusion of rewarding results for all. If you don't have money for labor, the first thing you must do is "fake it till you make it". In other words, create an illusion of power to make people feel as though you have the finances, knowledge, and vision. Create a vision of future success with the resources you possess. One person can create and start the vision, but a team has to complete it. A main level of hustle is to create a dedicated team by getting them to build your dream for you, but in the process allow them to live their dream to serve your will. This gives you free time.

There are 168 hours in a full week. Most people are employed 40 of those hours, which leaves 128 hours. Most people sleep 42 hours a week. This leaves 86 hours for leisure and recreational activity. 40 leisure hours could be spent on children, family and relationships, which leaves 46 hours on recreation. Recreational hours could be spent on exercise, skill building, or business research activities. This is equal to just as much time you use for employment. You could consider using these 46 hours as a second job working for yourself, doing daily research to build the career of your dreams. Remember time is an asset to be utilized just as money.

Spending Time

As I stated earlier "time is money" and when you were born you started to spend time. That's why time used is called "time spent or spending time". To me, being an entrepreneur is having free time to work on your goal. Everyone that is not spending time on his or her goal is wasting free time. The fact is we spend time doing what we want or don't want to do. Whatever you want in life is going to take time to achieve. Using your time to build your dream is time well spent. It's important to understand that time and patience are related in that they both require your respect and attention. You show patience by starting small and building. Respecting time is to have a regular dedicated schedule with your actions.

Free Money

The Grant Hustle

Grants are "FREE MONEY."A grant is just like a student grant for college. Grants are used for students to have an education so they can work and have a productive life. In the business world it aids in business economics. Grants are the government's way of helping to stimulate economic growth.

The Grant Program was established by the Federal Grant and Cooperative Agreement Act of 1977. It is money that is given to citizens from The US Treasury that you don't pay back. It is managed and distributed by the IRS. Truthfully this is just acceptable, expectable and respectable manipulation.

Important Note:
"It's Not Really Free Money!"
The Reason You Don't Have To Pay
It Back, Is Because It's Your Money.

The hustle Is that the IRS gives you a perception
that they are giving you money that's not your.

How Is It Your Money?

A Grant is just like a income tax return. You're a tax payer who pays the government money you've earned. The U.S. Government in return pays the IRS to manage your tax money you've paid. The government body is your business, so the IRS is employed by you.

How Does It Work?

The United States is a corporation that is owned by "you the people". The United States is governed under three branches of U.S. government legislative, judicial, and executive. You elect government officials to serve as the board members and directors of your United States Corporation as: the Governors, Senators, Presidents and Legislators over congress hearings so they can regulate your tax money. "The United States is your Corporation. The Government is the body of leaders that 'you the people' elected to govern your tax dollars and resources. Your Governing body hired the IRS as your accountant."

"The IRS Is Your Accountant & Watch Dog.
When Applying For A Grant You Are Asking, Your Accountant
For Your Income Tax Money To Do Public Service."

"Who Gives Out Your Money?"

Corporate foundations, government agencies and other private organizations are given billions of dollars each year from the U.S. Government to distribute to Americans through other non-profits for innumerable public reasons. They are like the middle man. Think of them as local income tax business that deal with distribution of your tax money. They distribute your money by rules we gave them the right to create

Here Are Some Well Known Government Agencies

Federal Level

Department of Secretary of State
US Department of Transportation
US Food and Drug Administration
US Department of Education
FBI - Federal Bureau of Investigation

State Level:

State Department of Transportation
State Department of Social Services
State Department of Education
Your State Economic Development

For More On Info. www. marcellusscott.com

Type Of Grants

There are many different levels of grants that are available to the public. These grants cover every kind of financial need. Grants are commonly used for Business, Education, Personal Needs, Housing and Federal Projects.

Type Of Grant Funding

Match Funding – When you or your business is asked to pays a percentage of the cost of the project you're needing a grant for, and the government matches 50% or more the amount.

Total Funding – When your government funds the entire program or project cost. In other words, when all the grant money is given for the project.

As A Citizen It's Your Right To:

1. Find A Community Need And Be A Public Servant.
Why? This is how you can become eligible for grant money as a citizen.

2. Forming a public committee on local or state level.
You can partner with your state, local governments, churches, or organizations and form a linked committee.

2. Learn Parliamentary Procedure
This is the rules, ethics, and customs that governing meetings. These are customary procedures on how committee and governing bodies are ran.

As A Citizen You Should Know:

1. Your city Is owned by "YOU" The people of the city.

2. Your city officials work for you. Mayor and City Council Members

3. You pay officials salaries by paying taxes, and by oath they agreed to do as 'you the people' say.

4. The government gives your city grant money for a community project.

5. The money Is controlled by your city officials for 'You The People' welfare.

6. If you're providing community service for the public benefit it is your right to ask or your money to help in the task.

7. You can also create new community projects under a non-profit committee or organization. To be voted on for use of your money

"Why Is Your Money Given Out?"

For Consumer need of Public Education, Business start-up or expansion, Real estate purchases, New Inventions, New Research, and Community Development Programs:

Reproduction - Childcare

Mental Growth – Education and Tuition Faith-Organizations Restoration

Physical Growth - Commodities Food

Shelter - Real Estate Land & Housing, First-time home purchase, Rent Assistance, Home Repair, etc.

For More On Info. www. marcellusscott.com

Employment - Job Training

Economics - Business start-ups / expansion Community Development, Inventions

Health - Medical Research

Who Qualify For Grants?

- **People with Low income or net worth.**
- **Minority Individuals** - People of certain ethnic backgrounds
- **Minority Females** - Women of certain ethnic backgrounds
- **The Elderly** - Senior Citizens Help
- **Small Businesses** - To Start Up Their Own Business.
- **Real Estate** - To Provide Housing For Community Benefit.
- **High School Grads** - Go To College and Start Small Business
- **Field Of Study** - Math, Science, Technology & Business.
- **Funding or Consumer Agencies**
- **Non Profit Business** – For FREE Community Services

Important Note:
90% of all Grant Money Is Distributed Through Non-Profit Businesses

The are millions of dollars that are available for citizens that a distributed by non-profit businesses. "The non-profit business get the large percentage of the funding." They are paid to sub-distribute small percentages within single disburses to the qualified that I listed above. Because of this, It's in your best interest to be a Non-Profit Business.

For More On Info. www. marcellusscott.com